Write that Book Now

Workbook

Julia A. Royston

B K
ROYSTON
Publishing

BK Royston Publishing
P. O. Box 4321
Jeffersonville, IN 47131
502-802-5385
http://www.bkroystonpublishing.com
bkroystonpublishing@gmail.com

Cover Design by: BK Royston Publishing LLC

ISBN-13: 978-1-946111-63-0

Printed in the United States of America

Dedication

I dedicate this to every person who has ever wanted to write a book. It's the topic, tenacity and the time that makes a book great. Do the work and the rest will work out. Let's go!

Acknowledgement

I thank my Lord and Savior Jesus Christ for giving me another opportunity to introduce more people to you. I thank you that you have entrusted this gift to me. Lord, let your Spirit move through this book to the people who will read it.

To my husband, Brian K. Royston, the love of my life for loving and cheering me on so much that I can be and do all that God has placed in me. I love you...

To my Mom, who is a great support and to my Dad who is in heaven but, I know is proud of me and always encouraged me to go for it. Thanks to all of my family for their love and support.

A special thank you to Rev. and Mrs. Claude R. Royston for their love and support of all of my business endeavors.

Introduction

So, you've always wanted to write a book? Of course, you have! I have written more than 50 books and excited to share my tips, tricks and talent with you on writing your first of many books.

Now, before we get started let me tell you that my company is here to help you complete and not just to start your book. If you get stuck, have a problem or a question related to writing a book, don't hesitate to reach out to me via email at bkroystonpublishing@gmail.com or schedule a time to talk at http://bit.ly/talkwithroyston We'll be happy to help.

For information regarding the Write. Publish. Promote Series from Julia Royston, visit: Http://bit.ly/writepublishpromoteitnow

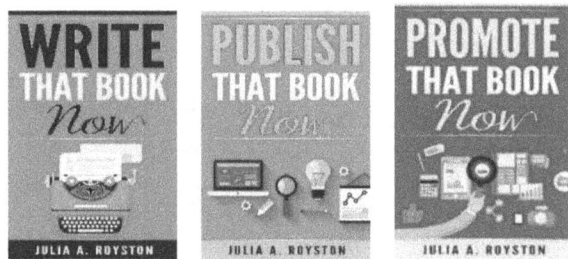

For the workbook, I made sure to guide the fiction as well as the non-fiction writer to starting and completing their book. Fiction is not harder, but a more involved process of writing. I enjoy writing fiction and non-fiction books, but realize that the thought process and approach to writing is totally different when writing fiction vs. non-fiction. As stated earlier, don't stay stuck, reach out if there is a question or problem.

We have wasted enough time dreaming, hoping and believing to be a published author. Turn the page to get started and definitely "Write that Book Now!"

Let's go!

Julia Royston

Table of Contents

Why Do You Want to Write a Book?

So, you've always wanted to write a book? Of course, you have! First, think, why do you want to write a book? Secondly, who do you want to talk to? Finally, what do you want to say to them?

These are just my top three questions that you need to ask yourself before writing a book. It doesn't matter if the book is fiction or non-fiction, which we will talk about later but you need to answer, the why, the who and the what of your book first.

Why do you want to write a book?

_____

_____

_____

_____

_____

_____

Who do you want to talk to in your book? Men, Women, Children, Young Adults??

_____

_____

_____

_____

_____

_____

_____

What do you want to talk to them about in your book?

_____
_____
_____
_____
_____
_____
_____
_____
_____
_____
_____
_____
_____
_____
_____
_____
_____
_____
_____
_____
_____
_____
_____
_____
_____

The Topic

What if you don't know the answer to the first three questions but still have always wanted to write a book? Then we need to find a topic. Go to Google and type in "Bestselling books." Find a list of the bestselling books that are currently on the market. This list will help you determine what books people are actually buying. If one of the topics interests you then, decide to write about it. Make sure that it is a topic that you have a genuine interest and passion about. Remember that once your book is published, you will have to speak about your book as well as remember the title and where to buy it. If the topic you want to write about is a topic on the bestsellers list and you love the topic, you are well on your way to writing a book that not only people want to read but are willing to buy.

What is the Topic of Your Book?

_____

_____

_____

_____

_____

_____

_____

_____

_____

_____

_____

_____

_____

_____

_____

_____

The Message of the Book

The message of the book and the topic of the book are different. The topic of the book is what you want to write about or the genre of the book. Fiction or romance fiction or self-help for domestic violence or even how to fix a sink. These are just some sample topics for a book. Inside the general topic of the book should be a message that you want to deliver to the reader. For example, the topic of the book is "Six Ways to Fix a Sink." The message of the book is that anybody can fix a sink with these simple instructions, step by step images and/or an instructional DVD. In other words, the message of the book should be related to the why of the book or the point or purpose of your book?

It should connect with you first because you have to be passionate about and believe in what you are writing. Secondly, there should be someone else in the world who needs that message right now. The reason I wrote my book "Write that Book Now" is because there are billions of people in the world with many diverse needs, problems and situations who want to write a book. I wrote the workbook because it will give structure and guidance to the book writing process. Wanting to write a book and actually working through the process to write are two different things. The end result of wanting to write a book should be actually writing the book. That's my message to you, "Write that Book Now!" and this **Workbook** should help you ***work through*** the process. Let's go!

What is the Message of Your Book?

_____

_____

_____

_____

_____

_____

_____

_____

The Outline

The outline should cover the topics that you want to discuss in your book. It's plain and simple. The topics do not have to be in final order or level of importance. The importance of the outline is to have a focus, guidance and structure for the actual things, topics or issues covered in your book

We discussed and determined earlier the main topic of your book. Now, we need to determine the supporting facts, issues and subtopics surrounding your book. I often give a very simple example of this with authors. If you are writing about Apples, what is about apples that make them special or that people should know.

For example, the variety of the many types of apples. The health benefits of apples. The history of the apple. The tastes of apples. The products that apples made from.

I have given you 5 possible subtopics, not in any order, that can be used in a book about apples. How many subtopics? I would come up with 7-10 subtopics. These subtopics will become your chapters in your book. Does that make sense? I hope so because that's how I have written more than 50 books.

In the book about apples, I wouldn't include oranges, pineapples or bananas, just about apples. In my years of working with authors, I find that with our incredible creative brain, we can think of so many things that we lose focus on the main topic. The easiest way to begin and complete a book is to be as focused as possible. The topic and subtopics in an outline format will help us determine what we want to include in the book and help us write it much faster and easier.

It doesn't matter whether you write out the topic and subtopics which will be our outline by hand in a journal, on a desktop computer or other mobile device, just get it down on paper or in a document. Others have suggested putting each topic on a note card. I sit down at a computer and begin writing my outline. Each line of my document should point to the one topic that I want to discuss.

So, let's go back to my example about apples. An outline of a book about apples could look something like the following

Book Topic: Apples

The history of the apple.

How do you grow apples?

There are variety of types of apples, red, green, yellow, cross bred, specialty apples

The health benefits of apples.

The products that apples made from.

Business aspects of apples industry

This is a basic, simple sample of an outline for a non-fiction or self-help book.

Under each topic now you are ready to start writing about the subtopic you have listed. For the 51 books I have written, I type out my outline first and then begin writing about the topic that is listed. For example, under the topic of the history of apples, write about it. Where did apples originate? Who was the first discoverer of the apple?

You don't have to write in exact order of the topics, just write what comes to mind under each topic, every day.

On the next page, begin your non-fiction outline about your topic you discussed in an earlier part of the book. If you are writing a fiction book, I will cover that next.

Non-Fiction or Self-Help Outline

Topic of Your Book

_____

_____

_____

Subtopic 1

_____

_____

_____

Subtopic 2

_____

_____

_____

Subtopic 3

_____

_____

_____

Subtopic 4

_____

_____

_____

Subtopic 5

_____

_____

_____

Subtopic 6

_____

_____

_____

Subtopic 7

_____

_____

_____

Subtopic 8

_____

_____

_____

Subtopic 9

_____

_____

_____

Subtopic 10

_____

_____

_____

Now that you have the outline, begin writing about the topics on the outline. So, if you are writing about apples, start with the history of apples and continue down the outline under each section of the book.

Fill in the text under each topic. It's just that simple.

An outline is a great guide and map to writing your book. Once you are finished filling in the blanks or writing the text under your outline topics, go back and read what you have written. It will surprise you how much you have written. These topics can now be transposed into chapter titles. You could leave the chapter titles as simple as one-word headings or adjust them to longer sentences later. It is your choice.

Write!

Fiction or Children's Outline and Profile

A children's or fiction outline is a bit different. Fiction writing is similar to writing for a movie, television show or play. Fiction is not in the same format of a script that is definitely required for a movie, TV or a play, but very similar in the thought process, sequence and flow of the book.

As we discussed earlier, a non-fiction or self-help book, your focus is a specific topic or subject. Examples of non-fiction may be 7 steps to a better life or Apples: health benefits that will change your life. The flow of these non-fiction examples may contain facts, figures, examples or chronological order of the steps necessary to the goal of the book.

For a fiction book, the book incorporates and contains multiple elements. The focus is the plot but for the plot to be clear, concise and entertaining, there may be several themes or spotlight on a particular social issue, character traits and relationship dynamics. The plot also takes into consideration of the setting, the characters, main and secondary characters, the time in history whether modern or historical, the language, the dialogue, the narrator and the visual imagery painted clear enough for the reader to see the picture with the words. Fiction is more involved but not impossible.

An outline is needed in a fiction even more than non-fiction. Why? Because you need an even tighter frame work and structure for the specific scenes or acts that you want to convey in fiction. The outline can help you begin the book, figure out what will happen in the middle and how the book should end. Making sure the book flows, makes sense throughout each transition and has an ending that gets us to a specific destination is critical. After the basic outline is determined, I also compile a profile of each character as well as the overall book itself. I will show you how to develop the profile once we have a draft outline.

Plot

the main events of a play, novel, movie, or similar work, devised and presented by the writer as an interrelated sequence. (www.dictionary.com)

What are the main events that you want to portray in your fiction book?

_____

_____

_____

For my book, Jillian, which is Book #1 of the "Women of the Fellowship Series," I started out the book with a flashback emotional scene with Jillian and her parents. The next scene brought it to the present-day situation and began to tell the romantic story by introducing the various characters and subsequent scenes throughout the romantic relationship. The plot are the main events of the novel. There should also be a goal of telling the story at the end. So, not to spoil the book just in case you haven't bought it, hint, hint, but the goal of romance fiction can vary. I like for my romance to end happily ever after but always with a twist. Another ending is for the romance to be open ended and the reader determine how it should end. Another option is for the characters to go their separate ways. So even though the plot are the scenes or events, the goal or results or ending of the story and the themes throughout the story can vary.

Simple Outline of the Plot of Jillian is below:

Girl has a horrible time in relationships

Girl has a horrible self-image in spite being highly successful

Boy reconnects with Girl from childhood through work

Boy and Girl work on a highly lucrative project together

Boy courts and woos Girl

Girl confesses that she is terrible with Men and doesn't think she is pretty

Girl has a jealous person try to sabotage her business and ultimately her life

Boy protects Girl

Boy expresses Love for Girl

Boy asks Girl to Marry Him

Police arrest the Criminal

No spoiler here - (Hint, buy the book to find out who is arrested and what happens at the end. Lol.)

On the following page, determine what is your plot or scenes for your fiction book? What is the opening scene? Is it scary? Is it romantic? Are they running from someone? Is someone dead and we have to find out later? I suggest to all writers of fiction that you start with a scene that captures the reader and grabs their attention. A slow opener of the book can cause disinterest and not a loyal reader.

Plot

What is the plot of your book? How will you reveal the plot?

Scene 1

_____
_____
_____
_____

Scene 2

_____
_____
_____
_____

Scene 3

_____
_____
_____
_____

Scene 4

_____
_____
_____
_____

Scene 5

_____

_____

_____

_____

Scene 6

_____

_____

_____

_____

Scene 7

_____

_____

_____

_____

Scene 8

_____

_____

_____

_____

Scene 9

_____

_____

_____

_____

Scene 10

_____

_____

_____

_____

More Scenes??

_____
_____
_____
_____
_____
_____
_____
_____
_____
_____
_____
_____
_____
_____
_____
_____
_____
_____
_____
_____
_____
_____
_____
_____
_____
_____
_____
_____
_____
_____

Setting

Setting is defined as the place or type of surroundings where something is positioned or where an event takes place. (dictionary.com)

What is or where is the setting of your fiction book? For my romance fiction book, Roberts Junction, I created a fictious place. It is deemed to be located in Southern Indiana in the United States but there is no such place as Roberts Junction, Indiana. But what are some very familiar places or landmarks in small towns in the Mid-west of the U. S.? Walmart, grocery stores, gas station, hardware stores, etc. The beauty of fiction is that you can create what ever you want to exist in that town. You need to determine and/or decide on the setting because even though your scenes may be the same, where these scenes take place will be determined by the setting.

Describe the Setting

_____

_____

_____

_____

_____

_____

_____

_____

_____

_____

_____

_____

_____

_____

Time in History

Now determining when the fictious book takes place in history will further determine and decide a lot of things about your fiction book. The culture, language, dress, behavior of men and women, technology and transportation. For example, if you are writing a book set in 1950 Southern U. S., using the words, Negro or colored to refer to African American people would be appropriate. In 2018, those words are considered derogatory. The time period in history must be considered. Additionally, with the same example, you wouldn't refer to the Internet because it didn't formally exist in 1950. People in 1950 actually had to go to the library to conduct research. Although, the government were using very large and cumbersome technology but not on a large scale.

What time period is your book going to be set?

_____

_____

_____

_____

_____

_____

_____

_____

_____

_____

_____

_____

_____

_____

_____

Characters

a person(s) in a novel, play, or movie. Dictionary.com – Who are the people in your fiction book? Although people may change over the course of a book due to circumstances, death, life, marriage or other changes at the beginning or onset of writing a fiction book you should have a general idea of your characters. Some questions to ask,

Who are the main characters in this book?

What do they wear?

What do they eat?

Where do they live?

What is their career?

_____

_____

_____

_____

_____

_____

_____

_____

_____

_____

_____

_____

_____

_____

_____

Major Characters

The book is yours and you can have as many characters in the book as possible but I suggest that you don't have so many characters that the reader is confused about the characters and the part that they play in the book. I suggest 4-6 main characters and then some sub-characters, side kick characters or minor characters that you may introduce mysteriously for 1 page and not mention them again until they have their own book.

What are the additional main/major characters

_____

_____

_____

_____

_____

_____

_____

_____

_____

_____

_____

_____

_____

_____

_____

_____

_____

_____

Minor Characters

Are there any minor or side-kick characters to the main/major characters? These people can play a major role in developing the main character, revealing the plot, maintaining and unveiling the theme or make take a major role in the next addition of the series or have their own series. I also like to be mysterious and write minor characters as the best friend which could turn on the main character, trick them or betray them in the end. It's my book, I write like I want to, but in your book, the minor character may and could play many roles. You decide because you are the author. Let's go!

Who are the minor characters in your fiction book?

_____

_____

_____

_____

_____

_____

_____

_____

_____

_____

_____

_____

_____

_____

_____

_____

_____

_____

_____

_____

_____

Theme

Plot is the events of a story; theme is the meaning behind or revealed by the story. Theme is sometimes defined as the moral of a story, though theme doesn't have to be a moral. Morals that double as theme include these: cheaters never win, honesty wins the day, and good guys finish first. How to Define Theme | The Editor's Blog, theeditorsblog.net/2010/10/24/what-is-theme/

In my book series, The Men of Roberts Junction, each man has suffered loss and abandonment. Although they each want love, my theme for this series, "don't let the baggage of loss weigh you down from the liberty of love."

What is the running theme of your fiction?

_____

_____

_____

_____

_____

_____

_____

_____

_____

_____

_____

_____

_____

_____

_____

_____

_____

Sub-theme

A sub-theme of the Men of Roberts Junction series is "hidden talents/abilities/knowledge." Clearly, it will make sense when you read the series. No book spoilers over here. The series can be obtained at

http://bit.ly/menofrobertsjunction

What is one or more sub-themes of your book?

_____

_____

_____

_____

_____

_____

_____

_____

_____

_____

_____

_____

_____

_____

_____

_____

_____

_____

_____

_____

_____

_____

Language

The language of the book is so key. I have to often caution editors when editing a book that some of the language is associated with the culture and time period of the book and shouldn't be looked at as grammatical errors but those grammatical errors could be the key to the book's story.

What are some key language nuances, keywords or phrases that your characters will use throughout the book?

_____

_____

_____

_____

_____

_____

_____

_____

_____

_____

_____

_____

_____

_____

_____

_____

_____

Dialogue

conversation between two or more people as a feature of a book, play, or movie. What is the conversation in the book? Who will be doing the talking? Will the plot, themes or setting be revealed via the dialogue? In my experience dialogue keeps the book going along with the action. What the characters say or don't say to each other is seen in the dialogue. Also, there is also inner dialogue in the mind of the character that may not be said out loud. Also, there is a format for dialogue that will help to make sure that major formatting will not have to be done after the book is completed and handed over to the editor.

There are times when key points are revealed in the dialogue. Also, all of the dialogue needs to be inside quotation marks.

Note the format of the dialogue in the example below which is an excerpt from Book 1 of the Men of Roberts Junction Series, Hank. Also, note the description that is after the dialogue. Also note the punctuation. Where does the coma go? Where is the period land and the double quotations go? Any questions, don't hesitate to reach out to me at http://bit.ly/talkwithroyston to schedule a time to discuss dialogue in your fiction book.

"Dr. Reed, I'm Annette Wilson, your administrative assistant," she said.

"Good morning, Annette. It is wonderful to meet you. You come highly recommended, so I am so glad that you agreed to stay on and work with me," Jasmine said.

"It's an honor. Your things should arrive shortly. I put in a request to the Vice President of Operations, and he replied that a crew should be here at 9:00 a.m. It seems that they have arrived now," Annette turned to Duane who was followed by two other gentlemen, Danny and Les.

"Good morning, Annette. You look wonderful this morning," Duane said with a smile, nod of his head and a wink.

Annette blushed at the compliment, "Thank you, Duane. This is..."

"Ms. Jones, is that you?" Duane cut Annette off the second that he recognized Jasmine.

"Duane Jackson, is that you?" Jasmine asked.

"Yes ma'am, it is. I didn't realize that you were the new Humanities Director. I just paid attention to the building and room number but not the name. Welcome to the Robert Junction campus of IU. Congratulations! We're a long way from West End Elementary School," Duane said.

"Exactly. I was thinking the same thing this morning," Jasmine stated with a smile.

"Well, we'll get your things moved in right away," Duane said.

"Thank you. I am feeling better already knowing that you are here to take good care of things for me," Jasmine said. Secretly, Jasmine hoped that Hank would be stopping by. Duane and Hank were best friends. They were as close as family, and they had worked together for at least ten years. If the past were to repeat itself, then Jasmine would soon see Hank.

"My pleasure," Duane said. The gentlemen moved the desk in, lamp, conference table, couch, chairs and cabinets that had been put together on the loading dock to await her arrival. She had shipped boxes with her degrees and other personal effects.

"Ms. Jones, do you want us to help you unload everything?" Duane asked.

"No, thank you, Duane. You can see that I didn't dress for unloading boxes. Can I get into the building tomorrow?" Jasmine asked.

"Of course, but I'll clear it with the boss and let you know," Duane said.

"Great, I'll probably come in around 9 o'clock in the morning. I'm an early riser, and I want to get the majority of things put away before noon," Jasmine stated.

"Fine, I'll let him know," Duane turned to exit Jasmine's office, and when he opened the door there stood Hank.

"How is everything? You guys need help with anything?" Hank asked.

"Well, no, but look who it is..." Duane wanted to call him boss as usual, but Hank waved his hand to stop Duane. Duane was confused but followed orders clearly. Hank was dressed in a blue work jumpsuit just like Duane, Danny and Les. Why Hank had changed from his oxford shirt, tie and khaki pants, Duane didn't know.

Duane opened the door wider so that Hank could get a full view of Jasmine.

"It's Ms. Jones, Hank!" Duane said.

"No, I believe that it is Dr. Reed, Duane," Hank said.

"I'm sorry, you are right, it is Dr. Reed," Duane said.

"I'll always be Ms. Jones to you guys. It's good to see you too, Mr. Simpson," Jasmine said.

"It's even better to see you, Dr. Reed. Welcome," Hank replied.

"Thank you," Jasmine replied.

There was complete silence. There were just two people staring at each other from across the room. Duane realized that he was no longer needed and closed the door behind him. He had a lot of questions and would ask Hank once he returned to the office.

Try your hand at dialogue below....

_____

_____

_____

_____

_____

_____

_____

_____

_____

_____

_____

_____

Emotion

With any creative outlet, whether it is writing, music, art, drawing, video, etc. it will ignite a feeling. I recently attended an author's book discussion and there was a full range of emotions by the readers. It was incredible. The author's book incited emotional outbursts, heated discussions about their opinions of the characters and their perspective on the why and how of the book's scenes. For a writer and publisher, it was incredible. I enjoyed every moment. So, ask yourself, what emotions do you want to stimulate or evoke in your book?

_____

_____

_____

_____

_____

_____

_____

_____

_____

_____

_____

_____

_____

_____

_____

_____

_____

_____

_____

_____

Fiction Profile

Given all of the parts of a fiction book that we have talked about so far, the plot, the characters, minor characters, the setting, the scenes, the theme, sub-theme, and the emotions you seek to insert throughout the text, what would be a general statement or concise Profile, not just the description but overall profile about your fiction book?

_____
_____
_____
_____
_____
_____
_____
_____
_____
_____
_____
_____
_____
_____
_____
_____
_____
_____
_____
_____
_____
_____

Children's Books

There are multiple genres of books and there are new genres being created each and every day. The two major classifications of books are fiction and non-fiction. Most books fall into one of those two main categories. Children's books usually fall into these categories as well but I wanted to point out a few things with regard to children's books. Make sure that the story or information that you are presenting will be in a language that children understand. Secondly, make sure that there are eye catching, colorful and appealing illustrations included in the book. No matter if the child can read or not, the illustrations, images and graphics will be able to help the child not only tell your story but create their own story. The imagination is so key with children's books. Additionally, children's books don't have to be long in length of pages. I suggest no more than 32 or 40 pages. If the book is being used or desired to be used in a classroom, know that teachers read a book over several days to cause students to think about they heard, reflect and even create other writings based on what he/she read in the classroom or in their private reading time. Review the earlier suggestions about fiction book writing in this workbook. Even for short children's books, think about the characters. Will the children in the classroom, homes or communities see themselves in this book? Where do these children live, how do they dress, what do they eat, what language do they speak and what are their dreams, goals and aspirations? Will this book inspire, ignite a flame for learning or support curriculum areas in the classroom? What is the theme, lesson or point of your book that you are striving to get across at the end of the book?

The same rules should apply to children's books just like any other fiction book. But, one key element with children's books, children are extremely impressionable and these impressions are long lasting. You can help support, encourage and feed the joy of reading with your book or reading can be a chore and never truly be appreciated even at an early age.

What type of Children's Book Will You Write?

_____
_____
_____
_____
_____
_____
_____
_____
_____
_____
_____
_____
_____
_____
_____
_____
_____
_____
_____
_____
_____
_____
_____
_____
_____

Poetry Books

Poetry was my first book. I journaled for several years and then one day, I started typing what I wrote by hand in these journals and compiled my first book. If you write poetry, I suggest that you have at least 50 poems written before you strive to compile them into a book. You can write as many poems as you like, but I generally feel that a good poetry book is approximately 75-90 pages and/or 40-50 poems should be able to accomplish that mission.

Your poetry book can be poems on various subjects which would be a poetry collection of poem on a variety of topics. If you write around a specific topic, pick one and assemble poems for the book around that topic. Thus, if you have 50 poems about love, compile a book of poems about love and then title it related to love.

What are the topic(s) that you write poems about?

_____

_____

_____

_____

_____

_____

_____

_____

_____

_____

_____

_____

_____

_____

_____

_____

Writing the Manuscript

You have the outline and should begin writing the manuscript immediately once the outline is developed and determined. If you are like me, you enjoy writing and don't find it hard to find the time or effort to write. Everyone is not the same and it may be your first book and your first attempt at writing a book. Here are some helpful hints for writing your book.

Schedule Time

Schedule time to write each day. Look at your weekly schedule. Determine when you get up, have to be at work and what your evenings look like. When do you have the most time to write? Is it in the morning when you wake up or in the evening before you go to bed? If I am focused on a topic, I write whenever I have free time, morning, noon and night. For you and your life, it might not be that easy. You decide but get to a time, schedule each day and stick to it. The book won't write itself so, you have to approach it like any other task. Make time for it. You make time for everything else and this is no different.

It has been suggested that you write for periods of time and then take breaks. These breaks cause you to walk away from the manuscript, rest your mind and body so that you can be more productive when you return to your manuscript. However, you do it, just do it. Write until you finish the book. The bottom line of finishing the book is to write.

Get an accountability partner

Tell someone that you are writing a book and let them hold you accountable for it. Get out your calendar and schedule times and days to check in with this person. Tell them your frustrations and possible delays in getting the book done. Let them motivate you and help you get the book done. You may even have to reach out to a professional book writing coach or mentor to help you stay committed to the process. That's what Julia Royston Enterprises does. They help authors get started and keep moving forward until they achieve the end result of being a published author. Reach out to someone who has actually written a book. They know the process intimately and can offer suggestions to help you keep going until you finish. No matter how long it takes, keep going until you finish. There is someone waiting on your book. Don't stop until you are done!

Commitment and Determination

As with any undertaking, there must be a level of commitment, determination and dedication to getting it done. There should be a sense of pride, courage, wisdom and faith in what you are attempting. No matter what that project is there will be distractions, physical tiredness, possible writer's block, family crisis and financial delays but be determined to get it done. I've had writers reach out to me who have wanted to publish a book for more than 40 years. I know why they haven't done it yet and that's because they weren't committed to doing it in the past. Because so much time has passed, they now realize that they don't know how much longer they will live, so they are more focused now than ever. Put in the work, stay committed to anything and you will reap the rewards for your efforts.

_____

_____

_____

_____

_____

_____

_____

_____

_____

_____

_____

_____

_____

_____

_____

Writing is Emotional

Your thoughts, feelings, pain, joys and experiences can and may be included in your book. Time after time, I have had authors tell me of the emotional roller coaster ride that they have been on while writing their book. The autobiographical genre brings out the hidden, deep, dark and sometimes extremely painful experiences in a person's life. I have had authors stop writing because they didn't want to face the past. But, I have encouraged them that they can't overcome what they won't face. Some of you might ask, I thought she was a publisher? I am but writing is emotional. Writing brings up emotions, and situations from the past that you thought you had conquered only to have them be revisited and realize that the pain hasn't fully gone away. Remember that someone else has and is experiencing that same pain. Your ability to live past your pain could be a message that someone needs to hear so that they can get past theirs as well. Writing is therapeutic and directly tied to your emotional well-being. Writer heal thyself through your writing. Keep writing.

_____
_____
_____
_____

_____
_____
_____
_____

_____
_____
_____
_____

Look for Opposition

In addition to the emotional impact that writing will have on you, the people around you will suddenly feel some way about you writing a book. Look for the opposition, jealousy, doubt and fear to come from someone close to you. I have written close to 30 books myself, helped more than 35 authors publish their books and coached countless others in writing their books, and it happens every time. Everyone is not going to be happy that you are achieving your goal of writing a book. You, who are reading this book will experience the same thing. The majority of the time, the person will be someone closest to you. I caution you to just be ready for it. If the person doesn't reveal themselves while you are writing the book, they will reveal themselves after it is published, the book is on a book shelf somewhere or you are selling it out of the back of your car. Jealousy, envy and sudden distance will occur from someone. It happens every single time. On the other hand, there will be celebration, motivation, support and sales from people that you didn't think would support or celebrate you so, look for that as well. It will surprise you who your true friends are and what family members have been jealous of you all of your lives but you didn't know it. Don't say I didn't warn you.

_____

_____

_____

_____

_____

_____

_____

_____

_____

_____

_____

Rough Draft

Once you have a finished filling in the text under your outline items then you have completed the rough draft.

Congratulations! Yippee! You have finished the first draft of your book. There may be more drafts to come but celebrate the first rough draft.

After you have finished the rough draft, put it away for at least three days. Don't look at it, review it or do any re-writing for these three days. You need time away from the book so that you can give it a fresh approach when you re-read what you wrote.

Three days after you finished the first rough draft, open the document or open the journal and read what you wrote. Read it out loud so that you can hear exactly how the book sounds to your ears through your voice. Don't edit yet, just read it all of the way through. Don't delete anything. Don't cross out anything and please, don't throw away anything! Just read it. Feel the passion in the words. Hear the emotion in your voice. Just read it. Put it away again and think about what you just wrote first. Don't jump right in at first but meditate on what you just wrote. How did it make you feel? How did it sound to you? What do you think that you left out? What do you want to add? Just think about the book first.

A couple of days later, open the document or open the journal and begin going line by line, reading it out loud again and making changes. This is called the re-write phase of writing the book.

_____

_____

_____

_____

Re-Writes

Re-writing is a critical phase after the first draft and should be seen with fresh eyes after the rough draft is finished. I find that reading a manuscript after I have put it away for a few days really allows me to be ready to do the re-writes. In the re-writes, your focus is to not start the book from scratch but to add any missing pieces or any other things that you want to say. Don't remove anything unless it does not follow the outline or isn't pertinent to the book. Don't delete it permanently because it could be the idea or important piece to another book but shouldn't be included in this first book. When you are finished with the re-writes, let it go to someone else. Let someone you trust read it to make sure that it makes sense to them and the message you were trying to get across was delivered. If not clear, ask them what was not clear and make the change. It is that simple. Just make the message clearer, don't delete or throw away the book. Criticism comes with the territory of writing. Don't let your emotions stop or block you from creating and delivering the best book possible. You put your feelings into the book but don't let your feelings stop you from moving forward to finish the book. I am the first to admit that I am sensitive about everything I create and want people to like it as much as I do. But at the end of the day, people still have to be able to understand what you wrote even if they don't agree. That is the beauty of writing. It is not that people have to agree but they do have to understand and get the clear picture of what you were trying to say in the book. There are books out there that are very controversial and do well selling in the marketplace. But a poorly written book is just that a poorly written book, no matter the topic.

_____

_____

_____

_____

Finish the Book!

Whether on a napkin, paper, tissue, computer or journal notebook, just write. No matter when you write, just write. There is no other way around it, just write and finish the book.

No matter how long it takes or what you need to finish, just finish it. Whether it takes six months or six years, finish the book.

Get the heart of a finisher and finish the book. There is nothing like finishing any project but when your book is finished, published and it is available online or on a book shelf, there is nothing like it.

Don't wait another minute! Don't delay another day! Write and Finish!

_____
_____
_____
_____
_____
_____
_____
_____
_____
_____
_____
_____
_____
_____

Do You Need a Coach/Mentor?

If you get stuck, get a coach, mentor or accountability partner to help you finish your book. Don't leave notebooks laying around for years without finishing your book. Get some help. There are plenty of writing coaches, coaching programs and free online tutorials to help you finish your book.

Visit www.juliaroystonenterprises.com or email roystonjulia@gmail.com for a coach near you to help you finish your book.

Sacrifice and Invest in Your Dream

To purchase a pair of shoes, dress, car or vacation, you make the sacrifices necessary to make that dream a reality. Writing a book is no different. You will have to make the sacrifice of your time, money and effort to make that dream of being a published author a reality.

There will be an investment that will have to be made when being a published author. Some of you may have to buy or upgrade your technology such as your phone or computer to make sure that you have all of the tools that you need to write your book correctly. All published books have to be in an electronic form before the publishing process can continue. Do you have the technology skills and equipment to make that happen? You may not now but it can happen. Go to the store, ask the questions, look into your budget and make that sacrifice and investment into your dream of being a published author.

You may need a coach to help and guide you while writing your book. Coaching is not free. Be prepared for the investment into writing coaching. Ask up front exactly how much each session will cost. Will there be a reduced fee if multiple sessions are purchased or is there a flat rate for each coaching session? How long will each session last and is the coach available for consultation in between sessions? In other words, can you reach out to the coach via email, text or phone in between sessions? That is an important question to ask the coach before signing on the dotted line of the agreement or making the first payment.

Writing Conferences, Retreats and Workshops

If you are serious about your writing journey before and even after becoming a published author, I suggest that you attend at least one writing conference, retreat or workshop. I host and attend a writing conference every year. These conferences offer opportunities to learn, network with other authors and publishers as well as receive guidance and possible critique of your writing. These opportunities and many others can be found at writing conferences, retreats or workshops.

There is a wide range of costs for these conferences so read the fine print for what is actually being offered during the conference. The fees can range from tens of dollars to several thousand. There may be a local or regional writing conference close by so look in your area. Your public library or writing department at your local college or university should be able to help you find a writing course or conference in your area. There are several national and international conferences held in exotic places and sites so, do your homework. In the past, there have been publishers who are looking for authors to sign to their publishing company and will review, critique and comment on your works for free. Publishers have nothing to review if you have not written anything, so write as much as possible. Outline the manuscript and have at least one chapter to be reviewed. The publishers are looking at the quality of your writing, the subject matter that you write about compared to the demand and sales potential for this particular market for this book's subject.

I encourage you to have at least a chapter written in your book prior to attending these conferences to be able to obtain a writing critique. There may be an additional cost for the critique but it is worth it.

Think Like a Boss

As stated previously, writing is a business. Take the business of writing seriously. Do your homework by conducting your own research. Ask as many questions as you feel comfortable with asking. If the person you are seeking to do business with doesn't answer your questions, move on to someone else. A book is like a baby, would you hand over your new born child to just anyone? No, so, don't hand over your book to just anyone. It's precious to you so, make sure that the publisher you sign a contract with treats your manuscript like the precious baby it is.

_____

_____

_____

_____

_____

_____

_____

_____

_____

_____

_____

_____

_____

_____

_____

_____

_____

_____

_____

Submit Your Final Draft

Once you have finished your rough draft, done the re-writes and had someone else has review your book who thinks it is good then, it will be time to submit your final draft to be considered for publishing.

Your book should be typed using a word processing software such as Microsoft Word. You can also use the Google Drive word processing software or Open Office word processing program to allow you to type your document. Your manuscript should have a 12-point font, preferably Times New Roman and not a script font because it will be changed immediately to a more readable font.

The manuscript should be double spaced and with a one-inch margin around the entire document. The one-inch margin should be for the top, bottom, left and right margins.

If you would like for BK Royston Publishing, LLC to review or publish your book, go to http://bit.ly/writeitnow and sign up to receive the Royston Writer Package. Once you sign-up, you will be directed to the Royston Writer's Package which is an informative package that includes the non-disclosure statement so that you have the assurance that your manuscript will be kept in the strictest confidence, a getting started guide to reiterate the formatting of your book, a memo regarding royalties and a blank contract for your review.

After you receive the Royston Writer's Package, email your manuscript to bkroystonpublishing@gmail.com and a member of the BK Royston Publishing LLC staff will contact you within 5-7 business days with further instructions on the publishing process for your book.

If you are interested in self-publishing your book, obtain my book, "Publish that Book Now" by Julia A. Royston on Amazon.com, Barnes&Noble.com, Kindle and NOOK.

We are excited for each of you on your journey to being a published author. If you need help, reach out to us, but for now, let's go and Write That Book, Now!

Initial Strategic Planning Guide to Market and Promote of Your Book

You have completed the rough draft of your book and possibly submitted it to a publishing company. This is awesome, but you need to begin to strategize how you will sell and market your book.

Some will ask, isn't this too early? My book isn't even finished yet? I don't know the title or have a cover? That is fine because in the next few pages we will map out a plan to market the book based on the topic alone.

It is never too early to be prepared to promote your book and to receive the possible sales of your book.

The next few pages are just a planning guide to get your mind, body and team prepared for the upcoming best-selling book. You don't have a team yet? Well, we are here to help you formulate a team to get this book promoted and sold.

What is the topic or subject of your Book? For example: Inspirational/Self-Help book about Relationships

_____
_____
_____
_____

List the top five best-selling authors in this genre or topic. You will probably have to do your homework and look up the bestsellers on Amazon, New York Times Bestseller list, etc.

_____
_____
_____
_____

_____

_____

_____

_____

What is the message of your book? The message of your book could be different from the topic. For example, the topic of the book may be about relationships and titled, "Domestic Violence: He thought he had me!" The message of your book may be, ways to get out of a domestic violence situation. Another message could be ways to spot an abusive partner as well as ways to not get into the situation.

_____

_____

_____

_____

_____

_____

_____

Name at least 3 Take a Ways/Hook - A take-away or a hook for your book is a point, issue, concept or information that you want the reader to remember. These take-aways or hook points can be the basis for talks, workshops or conferences about your book. Keep these handy for when any media outlet interviews you about your book.

_____

_____

_____

_____

_____

_____

_____

_____

What is the Target Date that you desire to have your book on the market? If you don't have a date, what is the best season for your book?

_____

_____

_____

_____

What is your scheduled time to write each day? If you enjoy writing in the early mornings, then other times of the day should be spent marketing and promoting.

Morning

Noon

Night

Early Morning

Who is your book's target audience? (Note: remember that you may target an audience with a book that does not appeal to that particular audience. This is a huge mistake for new authors. For example, if your market or target audience is men, make sure that the book's concept or idea, cover, interior vocabulary and marketing strategy is attractive to men.)

Men

Women

Young People

Children

Elderly

What social media outlets do you actively participate in?

Facebook

Twitter

Instagram

Periscope

BLAB

Pinterest

LinkedIn

Google PLUS

Do you have a website?

Yes

NO

Have you ever attended a writing workshop?

No

Yes

If not, go to Google and search for writing workshops that are held in the area where you live.

List at least 50 people that you believe would buy a book that you would write.
This list can be used later if you are able to compile a list of 50 people. If you cannot compile a list of at least 50 people, you need to expand your scope of influence in person and online.

_____

_____

_____

_____

_____

_____

_____

_____

_____

_____

_____

_____

_____

_____

_____

_____

_____

_____

_____

_____

_____

_____

_____

_____

_____

Notes

_____

_____

_____

_____

_____

_____

_____

_____

_____

_____

_____

_____

_____

_____

_____

_____

_____

_____

_____

_____

_____

_____

_____

_____

_____

_____

Notes

About the Author

Julia Royston is an author, publisher, speaker, teacher and songwriter residing in Southern Indiana with her husband, Brian K. Royston.

To her credit, Julia has written original music for 5 CDs, and 2 DVDs. She has authored 51 Books and served as a contributing author for 10 books. Julia and her husband spend their spare time overseeing the operations of 3 companies and a non-profit organization. BK Royston Publishing, LLC and Royal Media Publishing to provide quality, informative, inspirational and entertaining materials in the global market place in all media formats.

Julia Royston Enterprises is a writing and business consulting firm to assist aspiring authors and business owners get their message to the masses.

For the Kingdom Ministries is a non-profit organization that is established to encourage, enlighten and empower people to live the abundant life and walk in purpose and destiny. By profession, Julia is a retired certified technology teacher/media specialist with the local public-school system.

For more information visit www.bkroystonpublishing.com, www.royalmediaandpublishing.com or www.juliaroyston.net.

To schedule a meeting with Julia Royston, visit http://bit.ly/talkwithroyston

Get the Entire Write. Publish. Promote Series Today by visiting: http://bit.ly/writepublishpromoteitnow

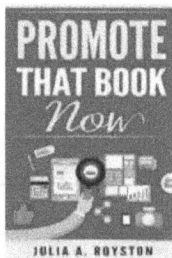